I0417676

*J*udy Leung is a writer, Communications and International Relations graduate and constant sufferer of itchy feet syndrome. Her passion for writing has been inspired by life's adventures. These include stints as an English teacher in Japan, flight attendant in the Middle East, and guest service agent at one of Australia's most exclusive resorts. She has a delusional dream to one day combine her interests in writing, travel and international politics in a paid job. In the meantime she happily writes about all sorts of stuff.

(c) Copyright 2011, Judy Leung, Sydney, Australia. All rights reserved.

No part of this book may be reproduced or transmitted in any form or by any means, electronic or mechanical, including photocopying, recording, or by an information storage and retrieval system -- with the exception of a reviewer who may quote brief passages in a review to be printed in a newspaper or magazine -- without written permission from the publisher.

Inquiries should be addressed to: judeleung@yahoo.com.au

The publisher and author disclaim any personal liability, directly or indirectly, for advice or information presented within. Although the author and publisher have prepared this manuscript with utmost care and diligence and have made every effort to ensure the accuracy and completeness of the information contained within, we assume no responsibility for errors, inaccuracies, omissions or inconsistencies

34 Pieces of Wisdom

Judy Leung

34 Pieces of Wisdom

This year I didn't have *another* 29th birthday. It was time to come out of the 20s closet and embrace being in my 30s. There's no need to live in triple-decade-related denial anymore because I've realised it's not so terrifying to be in one's 30s. An extra decade means more wisdom. In fact, I can think of 34 pieces of wisdom that life has taught me. That's one for every real birthday I've had so far…

Any life experience whether good or bad is valuable. Going through tough times makes you a stronger person and you'll appreciate the happy times more

*L*ife can't always be one continuous party. Shit happens. And so do great things. Treat the sad and lonely moments as one of many trials life throws at you. Survival is a testament to your inner strength and builds character. Celebrate and be grateful for moments of joy.

It's never the end of the world until it really is the end of the world. Gaining perspective helps when you need a reality check

*S*ometimes it feels like life couldn't possibly get any worse. It can. Watch the news and you'll realise other people are suffering from poverty, war, natural disasters, and political injustice. If this doesn't put your trivial problems into perspective then you're one self-absorbed individual.

Stop worrying about what others think of you. Do you like what you see in the mirror? How could you not? She's fabulous!

$\mathcal{W}$e waste too much energy worrying about what others think of us. What you think about yourself is most important. In the real world life isn't a popularity contest. Change what you don't like about yourself if it's possible and be proud of the person you are. No-one is perfect.

It's okay not to conform to society's expectations. Choose your own adventure

I say 'snooze' to tradition. Let desire and destiny guide your actions rather than someone else's expectations. Create your own rules but remember to use common sense in the process.

Confidence can mean the difference between success and failure

*H*aving faith in your own abilities can convince other people that you're capable and determined. Stand up straight, speak clearly and maintain eye contact. Believing you can get the job, the guy, the payrise, the discount or whatever it is you want is the first step to achieving success.

Money doesn't buy happiness, manners or good taste

Millionaires can be miserable just like the rest of us. Wealthy people can be exceptionally rude and often are the owners of hideous furniture and clothing.

Revenge isn't sweet. Instead, trust in Karma

You're a grown up now, don't stoop to the level of your nemesis by seeking retribution. Take the moral high road. The person giving you grief obviously has personal issues and is bitter and twisted about something. Rest assured karma will work its magic and their wrongdoing will come back to bite them in the arse sooner or later.

Laugh at yourself. Sometimes it's the best way to deal with the ridiculous situations you find yourself in

*H*eehee remember the time you made a fool of yourself at work? Haha what about when you were completely gypped while on vacation? You can't change what has happened so after you've stopped crying why not have a big belly laugh at your own stupidity.

13

Take risks. What do you have to lose? Your dignity perhaps but you'll get it back eventually

It's possible to go through life without taking risks but the journey is going to be pretty boring. Great accomplishments usually involve huge risks. Are failure and humiliation the only things at stake? What are you waiting for? Get started on your dream project. However, if re-mortgaging your home is required, take plenty of time to consider all pros and cons.

True friends are as rare as honest used car salesmen

There are facebook friends and then there are true friends. True friends will support your decisions and encourage you to follow your dreams regardless of how strange or silly these may seem. They never put you down or let you down and can be depended upon in times of real or imagined crises.

Food is delicious and life is too short to count calories. Just eat it

*B*eing health-conscious is good. Obsessing about calories, fat and sugar content can't be healthy though. Food should be a source of nourishment and pleasure, not guilt. Bon apetite.

Don't think too much. It can cause a migraine

It's exhausting to spend a lot of time analysing situations. Usually the result is a headache rather than a solution to your problem. We should think, but not over-think, before we act.

Travel is like a rollercoaster ride; exhilarating, adventurous, and often involves long queues and vomiting

*T*ravel may not be your *raison d'etre* but it can provide you with extraordinary experiences and should be attempted as often as possible. Not only do you discover a lot about other cultures, travel is a journey of self-discovery eg.you think you can't do the Inca Trek in Peru and go four days *sans* shower or porcelain toilet but actually you can.

When in doubt go with your gut instinct

*D*ecisions, decisions. Life is full of them. Should you accept the job offer, turn left or turn right at the traffic lights, or buy those shoes? Use your intuition.

Buying a second-hand car from a private seller without getting it checked by a mechanic beforehand is a very bad idea

*B*een there, done that. Bought an absolute lemon of a car and ended up having to replace the engine and tyres! Don't let the excitement of purchasing your first car get in the way of rational thinking.

If you have 'Mondayitis' on a Sunday morning it's time to look for a new job

*L*ife is too short (or too long depending on your outlook) to endure a job that's a source of misery. Start researching the industry you want to work for and look into further study. Work should be fulfilling. Afterall, you spend 40 hours a week there.

Perms are wrong. Don't let anyone convince you otherwise

*L*ike purple hair on nannas, perms neither look natural or stylish on anyone.

Life is only half fate. Follow your dreams and create an amazing destiny

Those who leave everything to fate are too lazy to take matters into their own hands. Great things don't just happen, people make them happen.

A little retail therapy never hurt anyone

*A*s long as you don't max out your credit card it's okay to treat yourself to an occasional purchase to cheer yourself up. You deserve it after that horrible week you've had.

Don't pretend to understand something when you don't have a clue. It could land you in a lot of trouble

If you're not sure about something, ask for clarification. Better to look a bit daft than totally mess up the task you've been assigned to do.

You're never going to be Australia's next top model but a good hairstyle, stylish clothes and makeup can work wonders

Knowing what suits your face, body and complexion can turn plain into pretty. If you don't know ask your friends or a professional for advice. The body is a blank canvas which can be transformed into a masterpiece. Okay, maybe not in your case. My point is, use your resources wisely and you'll scrub up nicely.

He didn't call you back? It's his loss not yours

*M*en can be arseholes. They can also be funny, kind and intelligent human beings. Don't waste time dwelling on the guy who never called you back because he's not worth it. You should be with someone that's considerate and the ability to pick up a telephone should be one of his many qualities.

Don't be afraid to take a stand against what you believe is wrong

If we all remained bystanders to injustice the world would be a terrible place. If you witness another person being mistreated or feel that you're being treated unfairly, say something.

28

Don't lie. It'll come back to bite you in the butt when you least expect

*Y*ou might think it's an innocent lie. Soon you're spinning a web of lies to cover up the original lie. Honesty truly is the best policy.

There's only one exception to the above. If you're late for work don't bother making up elaborate excuses. Just blame it on public transport and no-one will disbelieve you

If you live in Sydney you can always rely on public transport to be unreliable. This probably goes for most parts of the world.

Make that two exceptions. Not all babies are cute but you have to be extremely careful about expressing your true opinions

*R*emember: all babies including ones with jaundice, monobrows and moustaches are cute!

When you realise you're becoming your mother be very very concerned

Have you developed a habit of falling asleep in front of the television? Do you put a cardigan in your handbag every time you leave the house? Have you suddenly started spying on your neighbours? Seek help immediately.

Chances are you'll never win the lottery. Stop fantasising and start saving

It would be fantastic to win the lottery and be unburdened of financial woes. You could take a trip around the world and become a philanthropist. Sorry to break it to you, but it ain't going to happen. Better start putting some of that hard-earned moolah in a savings account to finance your travels.

Study is torture so make sure you choose something you're passionate about

Study is usually time-consuming, expensive and mentally draining. Don't study for the sake of studying.

Don't think of it as chucking a sickie. Consider it a much needed mental health day

*W*hy wait till you're coughing up a lung to take a break from work? Some of us never get sick and it's hardly fair we should constantly pick up the slack for those who do get sick.

**Equip yourself with persistence,
self-belief and determination
and almost anything is possible**

Talent alone isn't enough to get you where you want to be. However, if you add persistence, self-belief and determination to talent, then you're likely to succeed. If this combo fails, perhaps you should reassess your aspirations.

If life wasn't a challenge it would be boring

'Why does everything have to be so difficult?' we moan. Because if life was easy it would be boring, that's why.

Accept your age. No amount of cosmetic surgery can change it

Cosmetic surgery can reverse some signs of aging. But your age isn't going to change. And you're still going to have a wrinkly neck and wrinkly hands to go with your botox-smoothed face. Freaky.

Life should be 'lived'

There's a difference between living life and merely existing. Life is fragile and therefore we should make the most of opportunities which come our way. Live life to its fullest.

www.ingramcontent.com/pod-product-compliance
Lightning Source LLC
Chambersburg PA
CBHW070237290526
45789CB00004B/1665